ESCAPE ROOM PUZZLES
SPACE STATION X

KINGFISHER
LONDON & NEW YORK

Copyright © Macmillan Publishers
International Ltd 2022
First published in 2022 by Kingfisher,
120 Broadway, New York, NY 10271
Kingfisher is an imprint of Macmillan
Childen's Books, London
All rights reserved.

Distributed in the U.S. and Canada
by Macmillan, 120 Broadway,
New York, NY 10271

Library of Congress
Cataloging-in-Publication
data has been applied for.

Designed, edited, and project
managed by Dynamo Limited.

ISBN: 978-0-7534-7683-3

Kingfisher books are available for
special promotions and premiums.
For details contact: Special Markets
Department, Macmillan, 120 Broadway,
New York, NY 10271.

For more information, please visit
www.kingfisherbooks.com

Printed in China
9 8 7 6 5 4 3 2 1
1TR/1221/RV/WKT/120WF

FSC
www.fsc.org

MIX
Paper from
responsible sources
FSC® C116313

ESCAPE ROOM PUZZLES
SPACE STATION X

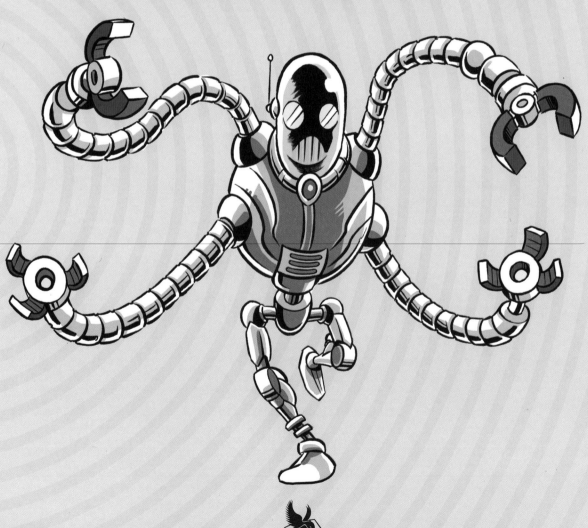

KINGFISHER
LONDON & NEW YORK

CONTENTS

MEET THE TEAM!

Hey! I'm Kiran.

Ethan here!

NAME: Kiran

STRENGTHS: Leader and organizer

FUN FACT: Loves extreme sports—especially rock climbing

NAME: Ethan

STRENGTHS: Math and science genius

FUN FACT: Amazing memory for facts and always wins any quiz

Hello! Zane's the name.

Hi!

NAME: Zane

STRENGTHS: Creative and thinks outside the box

FUN FACT: Loves art and takes his trusty sketchbook wherever he goes

NAME: Cassia

STRENGTHS: Technology pro

FUN FACT: Queen of gadgets and invents her own apps

WELCOME!

Kiran, Ethan, Zane, and Cassia always sniff out an adventure wherever they go.

This time, they are on a school trip to Space Station X when their day takes an unexpected turn. While the rest of the class are enjoying the tour, the friends end up on their own adventure.

YOUR MISSION:
Crack codes, solve sequences, and master mazes to escape every room. Help the friends get back to their classmates before anyone realizes they're missing. Ready, set . . . puzzle!

WHAT YOU NEED TO KNOW:

- Parts of the space station are protected by high-tech security systems. You are going to need all your problem-solving skills to get past them.

- Many of the corridors are patroled by robots and drones—and not all of them are friendly!

- The space shuttle home leaves in just 2 hours . . . and the clock is ticking!

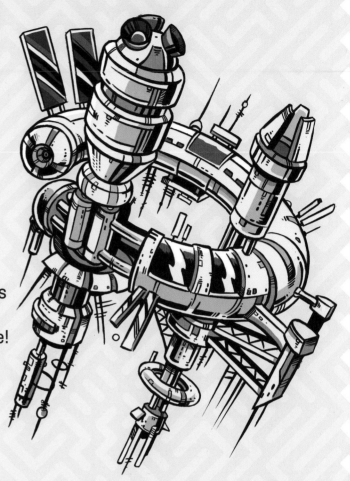

Important!

Help Cassia to keep an eye out for colorful symbols, like this (not including this one). There should be six in total! She needs to scan each of them into her tablet—they'll come in handy later on.

ROOM ONE:
DOCKING BAY

Cassia, Kiran, Zane, and Ethan arrive at the docking bay of Space Station X with their teacher and classmates. Before the tour has even begun, Kiran spots a door in the corner of the room with a "Top Secret" sign over it. Then she notices that the door is slightly open, so she decides to wander through and take a look.

Meanwhile, the tour is just starting. The rest of the class are busy finding out all about the space station. Ethan really wants to carry on with the tour—he loves all things space! But when he looks over to the door to see if Kiran has reappeared, there is no sign of her. There's no choice but to sneak away from the tour to look for her.

You all step inside the door to find Kiran. But as soon as you're all inside, it locks behind you . . . **and there's no way out!**

LOCKED BOX

Getting trapped inside a storage room was not part of the plan. As you all search for a way out, Kiran discovers a small locked box attached to the wall next to a square door. Could this be some kind of secret exit? To find out, you must first unlock the box. But where's the key?

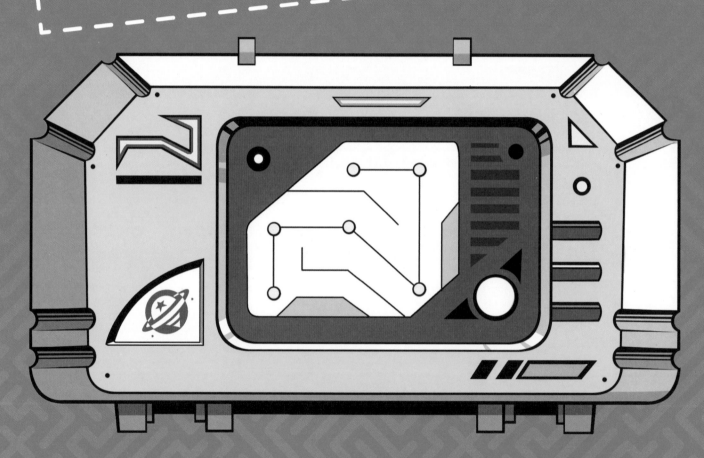

Ha! Ha! Ha!

What is an astronaut's favorite computer part?

The space bar.

Ethan spies a box of strange key cards on a dusty shelf. Perhaps one of them will unlock the box! Can you figure out which shape matches the lock?

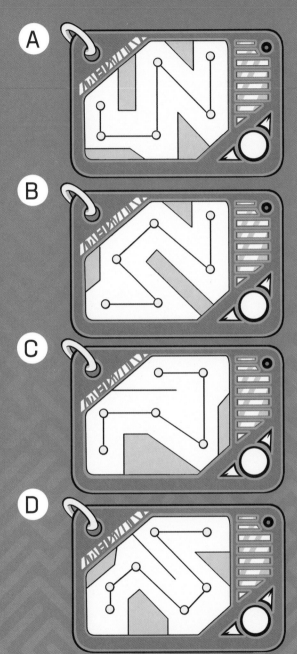

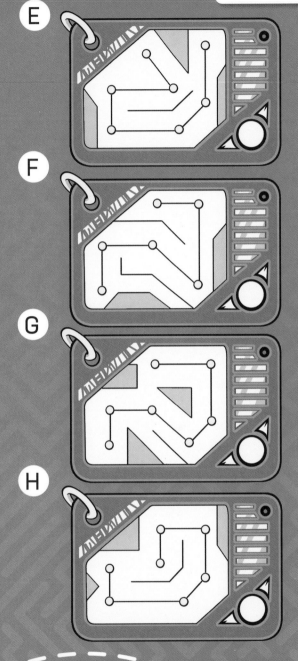

Nice!

The key card works! The box pops open to reveal a keypad inside and a small piece of paper flutters to the ground. There's something written on it . . .

THAT'S THE KEY!

The piece of paper has some password instructions scrawled on it. This looks like it's going to be easy . . . but not so fast! Read the instructions very carefully. If you get the password wrong more than once, the keypad will lock you out for good!

To reveal the password:
* Start on the red circle key
* Go down two keys
* Go right one key
* Go up one key
* Go right three keys
* Go left two keys
* Go down one key

Write the number or symbol of each key that you land on.

●	0	1	2	3	*
4	5	6	7	8	↑
9	@	↓	#		

You have two tries. Write them in the spaces below.

ATTEMPT 1

__ __ __ __ __ __

ATTEMPT 2

__ __ __ __ __ __

As the team figures out the password, Cassia notices an interesting symbol on the piece of paper and scans it into her device.

I'm going to scan that symbol. It might be useful for later.

Yikes!

That was a close call—but the password is correct! As soon as Zane enters it on the keypad, the square door clicks open, revealing a huge tunnel ahead. This must be the space station's air vent system. It looks like it's your only option for escape. Kiran leads the way . . .

MAKE A BREAK

You help each other climb into the vent. Can you find your way safely through the air tunnels and figure out which is the correct exit—1, 2, 3, or 4? A few words of warning: don't step on a grate or it will give way, and you must avoid the clouds of vent gas. If you breathe in too much gas, it will knock you out!

Grate   Vent gas

Watch out for the black squares, too—they look like loose tiles!

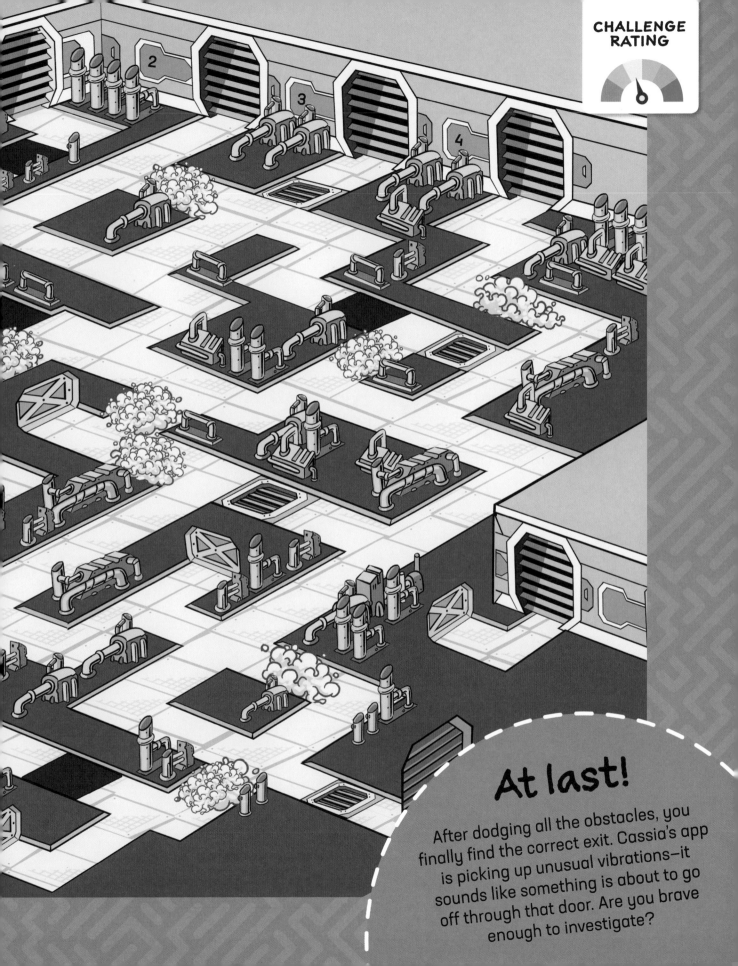

At last!

After dodging all the obstacles, you finally find the correct exit. Cassia's app is picking up unusual vibrations—it sounds like something is about to go off through that door. Are you brave enough to investigate?

ROOM TWO:
CONTROL CENTER

Phew! At last those dreaded air vents are behind you! But you still haven't found your classmates—they could be anywhere on the space station by now. The sooner you solve these puzzles, the sooner you can get back to them.

Unlike the air tunnels you've just escaped from, this room feels enormous. The bad news is, there's a loud beeping noise in here and it's making it impossible to think straight! You make a quick scan of the room and see a large computer screen in the distance, surrounded by desks and lots of high-tech equipment. Could that be where the beeping sound is coming from? It's time to figure out what's going on!

TO THE POINT

You need to reach that computer and check out the beeping, but the room is protected by some kind of security maze. Can you find a way to cross the floor safely and reach the other side?

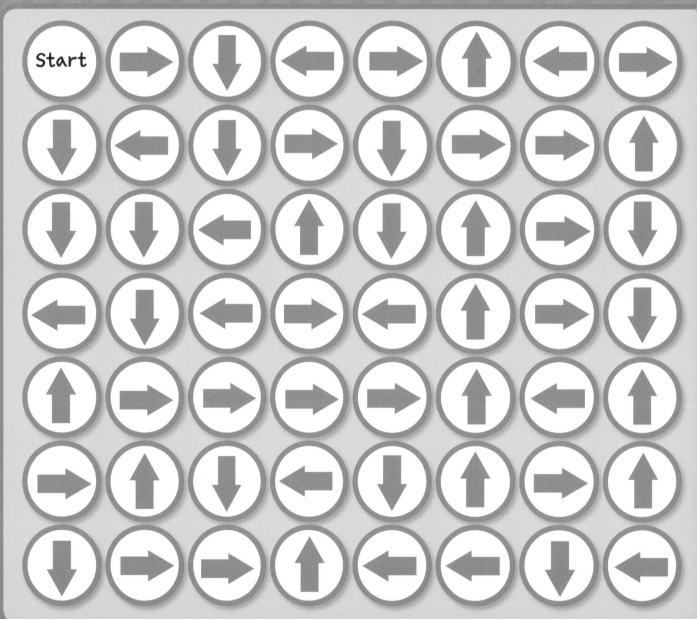

☾ SPACE FACT

Without wind to blow them away, astronauts' footprints on the Moon will be there forever.

One wrong move and you'll set off the alarm!

Take it slowly everyone. Who knows what might happen if we don't get this right.

On track!

Excellent—you made it through without putting a foot wrong. You know you're heading in the right direction because that beeping is getting closer . . .

COUNTDOWN CLOCK

At last, you reach the computer. A message flashes up on the screen: "WARNING! Low Power," and a countdown clock appears. There are lots of tangled cables coming from the screen and some need fixing. You need to do something—and fast!

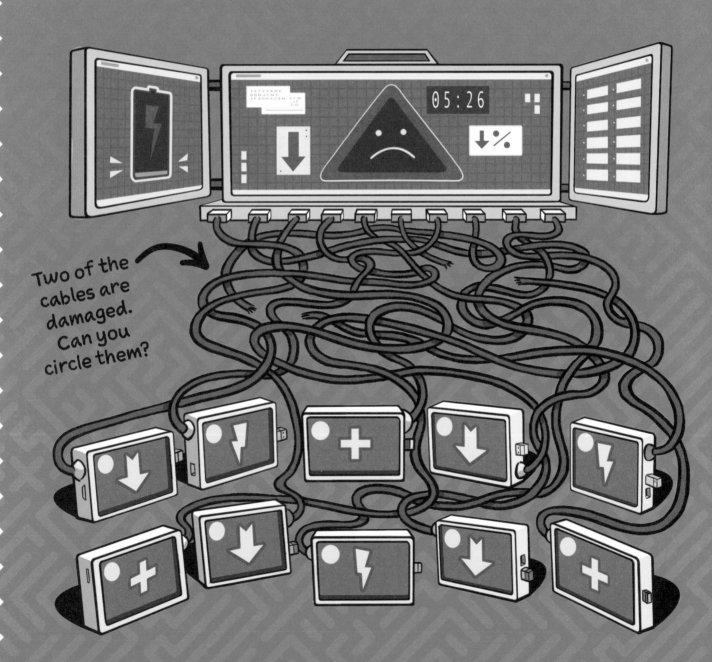

Two of the cables are damaged. Can you circle them?

You mend the wires and the beeping finally stops. The computer switches on, but another message flashes up on screen: "Data Error." Cassia finds a drawer full of memory sticks, but which one is storing the missing data? Read the clues to find out which memory stick you need.

Circle the correct memory stick.

Clues

1. The one you need is not pink.
2. It has more than one color.
3. It is not the smallest.
4. It has a symbol with 12 edges and 12 corners.

What now?

Cassia puts the memory stick into the computer and the error message disappears. Phew! Great work—you found it! So what happens now? The screen flickers and then . . .

LOCK PICK

A new message flashes up on the screen. It's asking for a password— talk about security! The password must be around here somewhere. Ethan searches the desk and drawers until he finds a briefcase tucked under a nearby chair. The briefcase is locked.

I bet the password for the computer is inside that briefcase. Why else would it be locked?

The sooner we get into that case, the sooner we can search the computer.

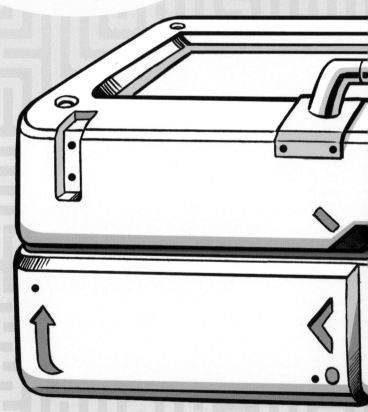

The password for the briefcase is four digits long. Follow these clues to help you figure out the combination for the lock.

4 8 3 7 — One number is right but is in the wrong place.

4 8 2 9 — No numbers are correct.

6 4 7 1 — Two numbers are correct and each is in the right place.

4 9 5 2 — One number is correct and in the right place.

Write the password here:

00:00

You're in!

You unlock the case and sure enough you find the all-important password inside. Zane calmly types it into the computer.

READY TO ROLL

Access granted! The password works and some dice appear on the screen. Kiran figures out that this is another puzzle to solve. Before you can go any farther, you must roll a certain number and color to complete the pattern.

Look carefully at the sequence below. Can you identify the pattern? Your challenge is to solve which color and number comes next!

1

2

3

4

Look! Another star symbol! I'd better scan this one, too!

This is so much fun! I can't wait to see what we have to face next.

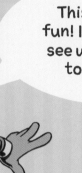

On a roll!

You complete the puzzle and another mysterious symbol appears on the screen. Cassia quickly scans it into her app, before a door in the corner of the room opens. It's time to move on . . .

ROOM THREE:
MEDICAL AREA

Awesome job, team! You've managed to unlock another door. So far, you've smashed sequences, beaten countdown clocks, and successfully escaped not one, but two rooms—basically, anything is possible!

Kiran takes the lead as everyone ventures into the next room, ready to face whatever challenge awaits. The room is filled with machines, medicines, and other strange gadgets! It looks like you're in the space station hospital. This is the place where the vital medical supplies and equipment are stored.

Ethan is desperate to play around with the gadgets, but the rest of the gang have other ideas. You're much more interested in finding your classmates as soon as possible! The school space shuttle leaves for home in two hours and you don't want to be left behind. You decide to split up and search for any signs of a possible exit. There's no time to lose!

BRICK BY BRICK

As you look around this new room, you notice a pyramid of symbols on the wall. Cassia scans it into her app and another message appears. It challenges the team to solve the pyramid puzzle.

I'll try out a few options in my sketchbook.

Look carefully at the symbols in the pyramid— can you see a pattern?

Your task is to figure out which shape should go in the top brick!

Ha! Ha! Ha!

What music do astronauts listen to in space? Neptunes!

☾ SPACE FACT

Roughly one million planet Earths could fit into the Sun. The diameter (width) of the Sun is about 109 times the diameter of Earth.

Hint
Pay close attention to the shapes in the rows directly below. How do they relate to the shapes above them?

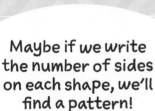

Maybe if we write the number of sides on each shape, we'll find a pattern!

Tip top!
The pyramid is complete! You all jump out of the way as a cloud of dust and debris begins to fall. Very slowly, the wall slides open to reveal the next room . . .

MAKE IT MATCH

You find yourself in a room surrounded by medical equipment. Zane makes a sketch of the scene and Cassia scans it into her tablet, but some of the details won't copy over. Can you make the image on the tablet match the picture in Zane's sketchbook by drawing in the 5 missing parts?

Hey, can you see that cabinet? It's got another symbol on it.

☽ SPACE FACT

The highest mountain we know about is on an asteroid called Vesta. At 72,000 feet (22,000 meters) tall, it is three times the height of Mount Everest!

CHALLENGE RATING

Matchy matchy

Excellent work, but it's straight on to the next task! Turn over to take a closer look inside the curious cabinet.

WEIGH IT UP

Cassia scans the symbol on the cabinet and checks inside it. It's full of medicine bottles! They don't look like they will be much help . . . or will they? In the corner, there's a pair of scales next to some sliding doors. To open the doors, the scales must balance exactly. One side already has a box on it, but the other is empty. Any ideas?

Look! Each bottle has its weight on the label . . .

... and the box weighs 124g!

CHALLENGE RATING

Your challenge is to find the correct combination of bottles to balance the scales.

Here's some space to work out the answer:

You did it!

As the scales balance, the doors slide open and you all walk through. You find yourselves in a small airlock, with two more doors in front of you.

SHAPE SHIFTING

Each door has a touch screen on it displaying colorful patterns. You must choose the correct pattern on each door to open it. But which pattern should you pick? Zane has a brainwave. The designs on the first door all look a little like the label on one of the medicine bottles in the cabinet. But which one is an exact match?

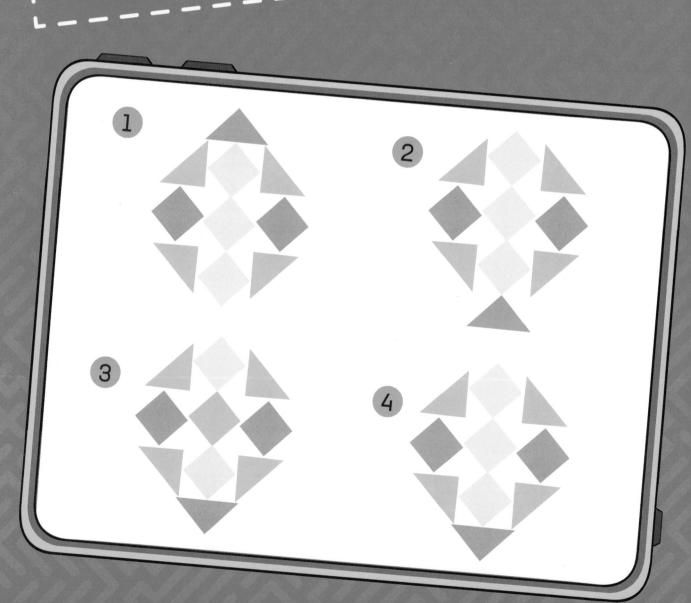

After tackling the first challenge, you move on to the second door. The screen shows an image of a tower and four circle patterns. Kiran thinks you have to pick the pattern that matches the view of the tower from above. Can you identify it?

1

2

3

4

Look! Another star symbol on the tower. Let me scan it!

Open wide

Good job! You've chosen the correct patterns. There's a clicking sound and both doors unlock. But there's still one big problem—which door should you go through?

WHICH DOOR?

Suddenly, two robots barge past you and stand in front of the doors. Perhaps they can help you choose the right exit? Cassia scans the handprint on each of their chests into her app. Immediatley, another message appears.

One door leads you closer to escape, the other one leads to a dead end—but which door is which? Two robots guard the doors. One robot always tells the truth, but the other one always lies. You can ask the robots just one of the questions below in order to find the right exit. Which one will you choose? Remember, you can only ask the same question to both robots.

Choose just one question to ask both robots.

Think very carefully before you choose. You only get one chance!

Do you tell the truth or lies?

Should we choose the green door or the yellow door?

Which door will the other robot say leads to a dead end?

Aced it!

It's time to wave goodbye to your robot friends. You exit through the correct door and move on to the next room. Who knows what challenges await you?

ROOM FOUR:
THE KITCHEN

You move cautiously into the next room, but it's a pleasant surprise! You've arrived in the space station kitchen. At last, the team can put their feet up and have a bite to eat . . .

Suddenly, the door closes behind you and everything starts to lift off the ground— including all of you. There's zero gravity! This is going to make things more interesting!

From flying food to dodging droids, you'll need to expect the unexpected as you make your way through the next set of challenges. And don't forget, time is ticking by. The school space shuttles leaves in just one hour—and all your classmates with it!

ZERO GRAVITY

It turns out that moving around a room without gravity is pretty challenging—especially when the air is filled with floating objects. It's time to grab some food—you could do with the energy!

Find all 10 food items and be quick!

Good find

As you float around grabbing food, Kiran catches sight of a big red button on the wall, next to another doorway. But where does it lead to?

DROID DODGING

Kiran hits the red button as she floats by and the door slides open. Somehow, everyone pulls themself through before the door slams shut and you all fall to the ground. Gravity has returned to normal! But what now? Cassia quickly checks her tracking app. It shows a system of corridors with doors on a timer—and they're locking one by one. Worse still, there's a troop of surveillance droids on patrol and they're not happy!

Start

Finish

You need to find the right way through the corridors before all of the doors lock.

* If you run into a droid, you have to turn back.
* If you come across a locked door, you need to find a new route.

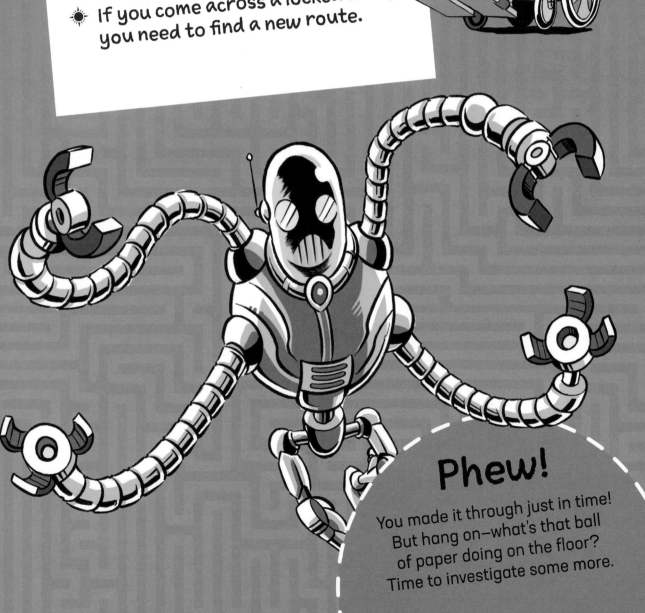

Phew!

You made it through just in time! But hang on—what's that ball of paper doing on the floor? Time to investigate some more.

RIPPED UP

The scrunched ball of paper turns out to be a collection of pieces torn from different pictures. Zane carefully flattens them out. It's clear that some of the bits belong to a ripped map of the space station on the wall. Can you identify the missing pieces so you can tape the map back together again?

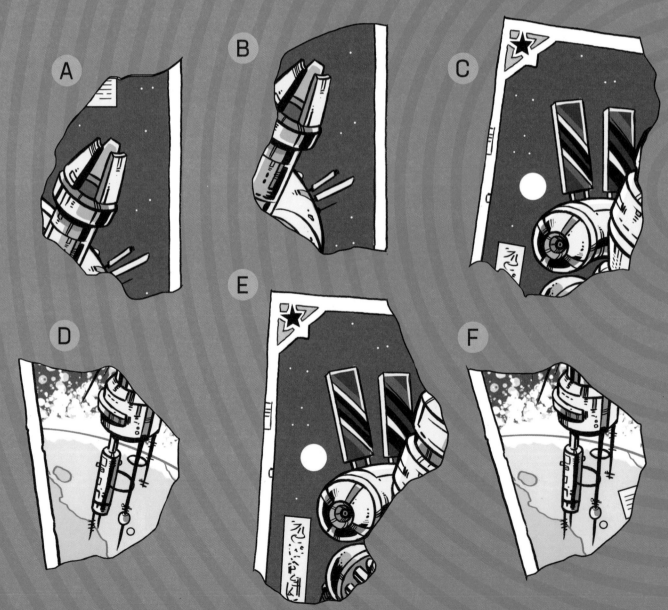

SPACE FACT

Unlike the sunset on Earth, the sky turns blue when the Sun sets over Mars! Fine dust in the Martian air makes the blue parts of the sky near the Sun much more prominent.

Fixed it!

The map is back in one piece and it looks like the team are getting close to the end. But hang on! There's more to this map than meets the eye . . .

ACCESS KEY

On the back of the map are four black dots and some instructions. You must connect up the four dots. Sounds simple, right? But there's more to it than that. You can only use three straight lines and they must not cross. Zane copies the puzzle into his sketch pad, so you can try out some different solutions.

Hmmm. Four dots, but only three lines?

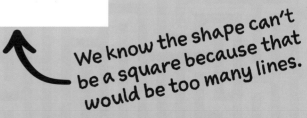

We know the shape can't be a square because that would be too many lines.

Use the space below to try out some different solutions!

ATTEMPT 1
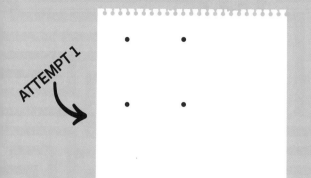

☾ SPACE FACT

The only planets that spin backward (compared to Earth and the other planets), or from east to west, are Venus and Uranus.

It looks like you have the solution, but how does that help you? Ethan notices a sensor pad on the wall, next to a door. When he touches the pad, the same pattern of dots appears on the screen. It must be some kind of access key! Very gingerly, Ethan traces three lines on the screen with his finger . . .

ATTEMPT 2

This is scary! I might only get one chance!

ATTEMPT 3
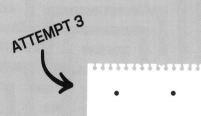

Solved it!

Success! The door clicks open. You all follow Ethan as you step through into complete darkness.

ROOM FIVE:
THE SLEEPING QUARTERS

Although you can't see a thing without any of the lights on, you are in the space station sleeping area. There's no time for a rest, though. There are plenty more challenges ahead!

In this final part of the escape challenge, you'll need to find ways to go undetected as you face droids and robots. Remember—this is the final push. You are so close now and the last thing that you want is to get stopped at this stage.

By now you should have spotted five symbols. Cassia has been scanning them into her app as you go—she had a feeling they would be needed at some point! There should be six in total, so keep your eyes peeled for the last one. The shuttle home leaves in just half an hour!

SEQUENCES

Kiran flicks a light switch, but nothing happens. The lights are password controlled. Luckily, the password is written under the switch. The only problem is, the last digit is missing. Can you solve what the missing number is? To ace this challenge, you must first figure out what the pattern is.

2   3   5   9   17   33   ——

Choose from these four options:

42   55   65   71

Maybe it has something to do with the gaps between the numbers...

SPACE FACT

If it was possible to fly to Pluto, it would take over 800 years. The dwarf planet is over 3 billion miles (5 billion kilometers) away from Earth!

Use this piece
of paper to work
out the answer.

Everyone, wait up.
I've got to scan
that symbol, too!

Can you find a pattern?

Ha! Ha! Ha!

What is an astronaut's
favorite chocolate?

Milky Way!

Got it?

Of course you did!
Puzzle solved and another
colorful shape scanned
into the app. Well done!

POD SPOT

Finally, the lights turn on and you can look around. The sleeping area is packed with pods. At first glance, they all look identical, but look more closely. One of them is different. Can you detect which?

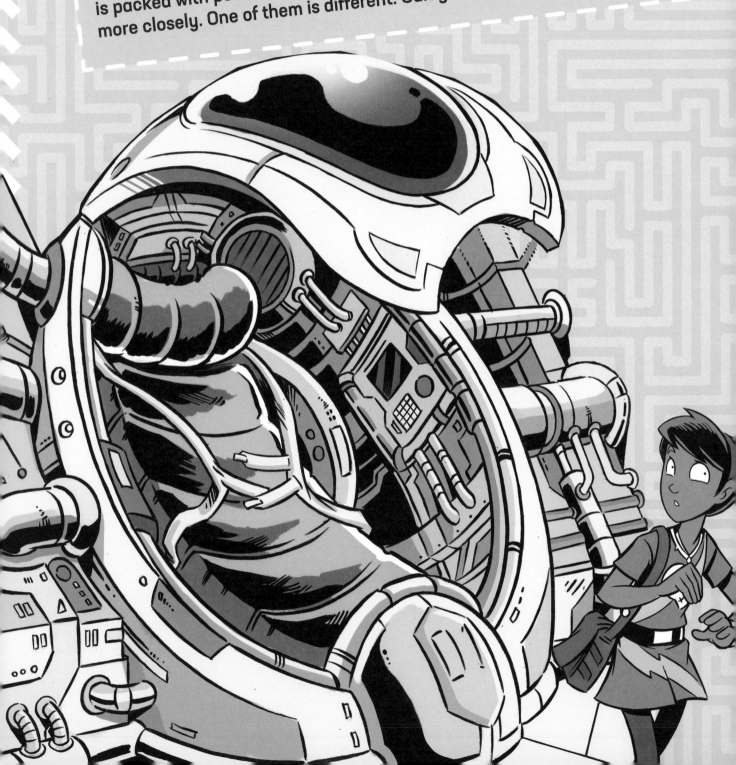

☾ SPACE FACT

In space there is no such thing as "up" or "down" because the lack of gravity allows people to move in any direction. Astronauts must secure themselves to their beds to stop them from floating all over the place as they sleep.

1
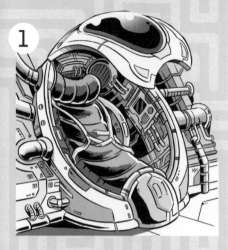

2

3

4
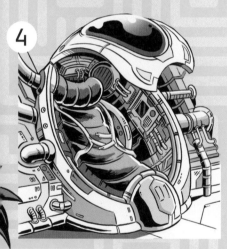

5

6
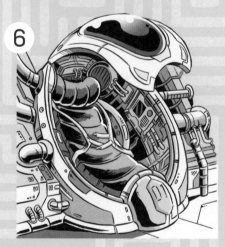

Awesome!

You've found the odd pod out. Everyone huddles around to take a closer look, then . . . oops! Zane accidentally knocks a button on the side of the pod and an alarm goes off!

Oops! Sorry about that, team!

SPACE SUDOKU

A robot appears from nowhere! It has a computer screen for a face, which beeps loudly as it turns on. Zane takes a closer look at the screen. There's a sudoku grid filled with shapes, but it's not complete. Your challenge is to finish the grid of shapes.

We have to arrange all of these images in the grid to fill in the blanks.

🌙 SPACE FACT

The International Space Station orbits Earth 16 times a day, passing through 16 sunrises and sunsets.

54

You can either draw or write to complete the grid.

Each picture must only appear once in each column, row, and square.

Great job!

Challenge successfully completed, but the robot has yet another puzzle to test you . . .

HIDDEN MESSAGE

After completing the sudoku grid, two rows of squares appear on the robot's screen. The team take a closer look. It's a sequence to complete. Your task is to identify what comes next in the top row. There are five options to choose from.

The lines in the squares must represent something— but what?

Ha! Ha! Ha!

How do you throw a party in space? You planet!

Choose one of the yellow squares to complete the sequence.

①   ②   ③   ④   ⑤

Let it slide!

As soon as the sequence is complete, the screen turns green and the robot slides to the left to reveal . . . another exit! But what, or who, will you discover on the other side?

GO UNDETECTED

On the other side, you come face to face with an army of security drones and there's only one way to get by them. The drones are programmed to recognize only one of these suits as their boss. Can you figure out which suit Kiran should wear so she can persaude the drones to let the team by?

☽ SPACE FACT

Older rockets used to only be good for a single flight, but today's rockets are built to be reuseable. Stages of the rocket that fall away are recovered on Earth and refurbished, ready to be used again.

Study the drone carefully. Is there anything that the drone has in common with one of the suits?

Epic!

Now that Kiran has the right suit to wear, the drones give you no problems. Completing your final challenge is in sight!

SAFE ROUTE

You're almost there! To get through this last area, you'll need to stay alert. Cassia brings up the symbols she scanned and a map of corridors appears on her tablet. Could the symbols be the key to finding the way out of here? Be warned, the corridors are littered with sensors—step on one of them and you'll be ejected into space.

Start

Are you ready to face the final challenge?

Number the 6 star symbols in the panel below in the order you found them during your space adventure. Then follow the stars through the maze from first to last to find the only safe route. Be careful not to set off the security sensors!

___ ___ ___

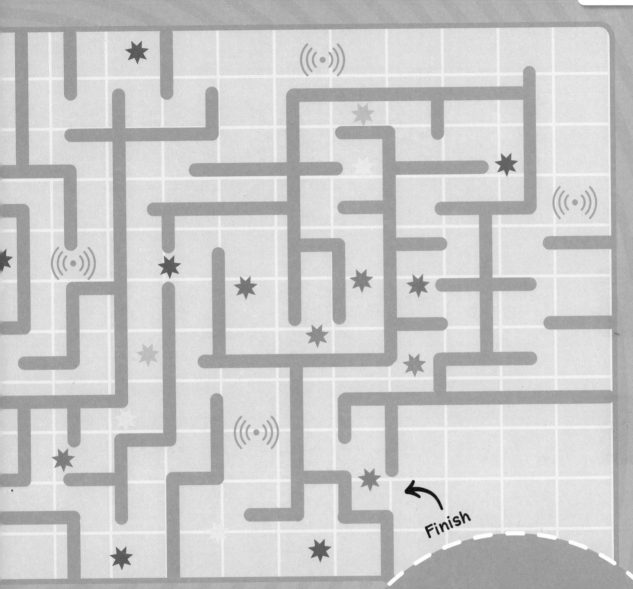

Finish

You did it!

You find yourselves back in the docking bay . . . you made it! Ethan catches sight of the tour guide with the rest of the class—and the shuttle home is just about to leave! You may have missed the tour, but you have just explored Space Station X! Will anyone ever believe the adventure you've been on?

ANSWERS

PAGES 10-11
Keycard F will unlock the box.

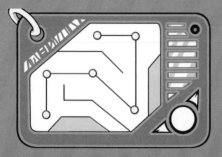

PAGES 12-13
KEY: 9 @ 5 8 6 ↓

PAGES 14-15

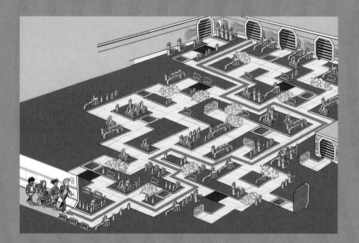

PAGES 18-19

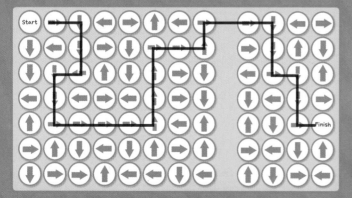

PAGES 20-21

PAGES 22-23
PASSWORD: 6 3 5 1

PAGES 24-25

 3 is the correct dice.
There is a six, one and four on each
line and there should be two orange
dice and one purple die. The missing
die is an orange number one.

PAGES 28-29

PAGES 30-31

PAGES 32-33
Select bottles with these weights:
25g, 18g, 20g, 12g, 32g, 17g

PAGES 34-35

 Pattern 4 is the correct pattern.

 Capsule 4 is the correct capsule.

PAGES 36-37

The correct question is: "Which door will the other robot say leads to a dead end?"

If you ask this question, it won't matter which robot is which—they will both say the same thing. The robot that tells the truth will tell you what the liar will say. The robot that tells lies will lie about what the truthful robot would say and tell you the wrong door. So they will both tell you the door that leads to the dead end! So you pick the other door.

PAGES 40-41

PAGES 42-43

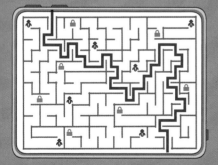

PAGES 44-45

1: **E**   2: **B**   3: **F**

PAGES 46-47

PAGES 50-51

2 3 5 9 17 33 **65**
The sum of the gap between the numbers doubles each time.

PAGES 52-53

Pod 5 is the odd one out.

PAGES 54-55

PAGES 56-57

PAGES 58-59

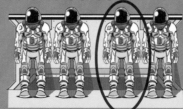

PAGES 60-61

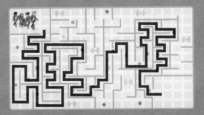

SEE YOU ON THE NEXT ADVENTURE!

Color in the team!